NUMBER 715

THE ENGLISH EXPERIENCE

ITS RECORD IN EARLY PRINTED BOOKS PUBLISHED IN FACSIMILE

(EDMUND BOLTON)
THE CITIES ADVOCATE
LONDON, 1629

WALTER J. JOHNSON, INC.
THEATRUM ORBIS TERRARUM, LTD.
AMSTERDAM 1975 NORWOOD, N.J.

The publishers acknowledge their gratitude to
the Curators of the Bodleian Library, Oxford,
for their permission to reproduce the Library's
copy, Shelfmark: Wood 590 (2).

S.T.C. No. 3219

Collation: A^4, a^4, $B-I^4$

Published in 1975 by

Theatrum Orbis Terrarum, Ltd.
Keizersgracht 526, Amsterdam

&

Walter J. Johnson, Inc.
355 Chestnut Street
Norwood, New Jersey
07648

Printed in the Netherlands

ISBN: 90 221 0715 9

Library of Congress Catalog Card Number
74-28834

THE
CITIES
ADVOCATE,

IN THIS CASE OR QVE-
ſtion of Honor and Armes;

Whether Apprentiſhip extinguiſheth Gentry?

Containing a cleare Refutation of the perni-
cious common errour affirming it, ſwal-
lowed by *Eraſmus* of *Roterdam*, Sir *Thomas*
Smith in his Common-weale, Sir *Iohn*
Fern in his Blazon, *Raphe Broke*
Yorke Herald, and others.

With the Copies or Tranſcripts of three Letters which
gaue occaſion of this worke.

Lam, Ierem. cap. 3. ver. 27.
Bonum eſt viro cum portauerit jugum ab adoleſcentia ſua.

LONDON,
Printed for *William Lee*, at the Signe of the Turkes Head
next to the Miter and Phœnix in *Fleet-ſtreet.*

Monſieur FLORENTIN *de* THIERRIAT,
Eſcuyer, Seigneur de LOCHEPIERRE, LON-
GVET, SAINCT NAVOIR, RAON AV
BOYS, *&c.*

De la Nobleſſe de Race, *Num.* 99.

En matiere de Nobleſſe il faut obſeruer la Couſtume du lieu, et les mœurs des peuples ; dautant que les uns eſtiment une choſe honneſte et Noble que les autres tiennent pour ſordide et diſhonneſte.

Num. 118.

Les choſes que derogent a la Nobleſſe, qu'il faut touſiours meſurer, ſur les Couſtumes des lieux, parce qu'un peuple approuue ſouuent un exercice pour honneſte, qu'un autre defend et prohibe comme ſordide, et uicieux au Gentilhomme.

HONORATISSIMO

SENATVI
POPVLO
QVE,
AVGVSTÆ VRBIS
LONDINEN-
SIS.

A 2

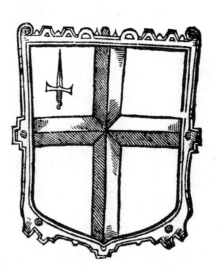

RIGHT HONORABLE:

He Author of this work, ſtyling himſelfe accor-ding to the nature of his part therein T H E C I T I E S A D V O-c a t e, after tenne, or twelue yeares ſpace from the firſt date of the accompliſhment, reſoluing at laſt to permit the edition, doth reuerently here aduance and preſent to the ho-norable good acceptance of your Lord-ſhip, of all the L ords, and other the wor-thy perſons, to whom, in the qualitie of the cauſe, the conſideration reacheth; *The cleare refutation of that peſtilent er-ror, which hauing ſome authority for it,*

A 3   *and*

and many iniurious partakers, layes vpon the hopefull, and honeſt eſtate of APPREN-TISHIP *in* LONDON, *the odious note of bondage, and the barbarous penaltie of loſſe of Gentry* : to the great reproach of our Kingdomes policie, and to the manifold damage of the publike. In this one act of his, the Aduocate therefore doth not onely ſeeme to be the Patron or Defen-dor of birth-rights, and of the rights of fortunes, but the Champion alſo of ciuill Arts, & of flouriſhing Induſtrie among you: the ſinewes, and life it ſelfe of Com-mon-weale. The occaſion which indu-ced him to enter the liſts ſingle againſt a multitude, in this good quarrell, was priuate, as appeares by the Letters at the end of the worke, but the cauſe, is abſo-lutely ſuch (according to his beſt vn-derſtanding)as he ſhould not refuſe to a-bett & ſecond with his ſword, the ſtrokes of his pen, to that purpoſe. For, though the

the Schooles, and Camp, are moſt proper for Honor and Armes, yet the ancient wiſedome, and the like ancient boun-
ty of our Sages, did euer leaue the gates
of Honor open to City-Arts, and to
the myſteries of honeſt gaine, as fun-
damentall in Common-weale, and ſuſ-
ceptiue of externall ſplendor: according
to the moſt laudable examples of riſing
Rome, vnder her firſt Dictators, & Conſuls. By which their ſuch moderation
and iudgement, they happily auoided
two oppoſite rockes; tyrannicall appro-
priation of Gentry to ſome certaine old
families, as in *Germanie,* and the confuſi-
on of allowing hereditarie Nobleneſſe,
or Gentry, to none at all, as vnder the
Sultan, in *Turkey.* With how true and
entire a good will this free ſeruice is per-
formed by the Author may eaſily be ga-
thered from hence, that hee willingly
giues the obliuion of his owne name in-

to

to the merit; conſcience of the fact, ſuf-
ficing. Now, for him to informe your
Lordſhips and the reſt (out of the title
de origine iuris, in *Cæſarean* Lawes) how
the noble people of oldeſt *Rome* accep-
ted the booke which *Gnæus Flauius* dedicated to their name, and vſes, what
were it elſe, but inofficiouſly to dictate
your part, and not humbly to offer his
owne; which neuertheleſſe here he moſt
officiouſly doth, being truly able to ſay,
vpon his owne behalfe, that he hath pur-
loined no mans labours (as that *Flauius*
did) but is through all the true and
proper owner.
The Author is your
humble ſeruant,
Valete in Chriſto Jeſu.

XI. *Cal. November.* CIƆ CI CXXVIII.

To the Gentlemen of ENGLAND
in generall.

BE not *displeased with this bold enterprise, as if it were in fauour of the euill manners of a multitude, who passe vnder the title of* APPRENTISES. *For neither the incorrigibly vicious, who are pestilent to morall and ciuill vertue; nor the incorrigibly forgetfull of their betters, whom insolencie maketh odious, haue any part herein at all. For first, it wholly belongs to such, among masters, or Citizens as are generously disposed, & worthily qualifide, men who say with* Publius Syrus,

Damnum appellandum est cum mala fama lucrũ; *and then to such among Apprentises, as resemble* Puti-phars *chaste* Ioseph, *or Saint* Pauls *conuerted* One-simus; *yongmen, who say (with* Statius Cæcilius, *in his* Plotius)

Libere seruimus, salua vrbe, atque arce, *meaning by the* Citie, *and the* Citadel, *the bodie and the head of man.*

Valete.

a   To

To the happie Masters of Laudable
Apprentises in LONDON.

RIght worthy Citizens, you shal not for this worke finde your honest seruants the lesse seruiceable, but the more. For, in good bloods, and good natures, praise, and honor preuaile aboue rigour and blowes. And because your selues, for the most part, were Apprentises once, you may therefore behold herein, with comfort, the honesty of your estate when you were such, and the splendour of what you are now in right. The vnthankefull (if any such should happen to rankle among you) may be warn'd; that the iuyce of Ingratitude doth forfeit libertie, and that they are truly bondmen; if not according to the letter, nor in their proper condition, yet according to the figuratiue sense, and in their improper baseneffe.

VALETE.

TO
THE MODEST APPREN-
tifes of LONDON, Schollars, and
Difciples in Citie-Arts, during their
feuen or more yeares Nouicefhip.

He princ:pall obiection againft publifh-
ing either this or any other booke of
like argument, hath alwayes beene
grounded(by the moft wife and noble)
vpon a feare, that the infolencies of the
youth, and irregular frie of the Ci-
tie, would thereby take encreafe : which hauing heretofore beene intollerable (in common pollicie) and in no
little meafure fcandalous to the Kingdome, were hatefull
to cherifh, or to giue the leaft way vnto. But it hath alrea-
die beene elfewhere anfwered; that thofe Apprentifes are
of the dreggs, and branne of the vulgar : fellowes voyd of
worthy blood, and worthy breeding, and (to fpeake with
fit freedome) no better then meerly rafcall; the ordinary
balls, plaid (by the hand of Iuftice) into the *Bridewells*,
in or about the Citie : yea perhaps, not Apprentifes at all,
but forlorne companions, mafterleffe men, tradeleffe, and
the like, who preying for mifchiefe, and longing to doe it,
are indeed the very Authors of all that is vile; difcourte-
ous to honorable (all trauelling ftrangers ought to be generally vfed as fuch) rude towards Natiues, feditious
among their owne, and villanous euerywhere. But
you (none of that caitiue and vntruftie number) are the
parties,

parties, for whom this labour hath been vndergone, whose behauiours (full of gentlenesse, and of bounden dutie to superiors) commend you to the present times, and maintaine in you that stocke of good hope, out of which are in due time elected those successions of the whole, which make the politicall bodie or state of a Citie immortall. Thinke therefore with your selues, that by how much this most friendly office tends to your more defence, and praise, by so much you are the more bound to beare your selues honestly, and humbly. In your so doing, the Citie of *London*, which (before *Rome* it selfe was built) was rockt in a *Troian* Cradle, by the founder, and Father thereof (as the most ancient extant monuments, setting all late phansies aside, beare witnesse) heroicke *Brute*, or *Brytus*; vnder *Claudius Cæsar*, the Metropolis of the *Trinobants* ; vnder other *Cæsars* afterwards, *Augusta*, or the maiesticall Citie ; which, for hugenesse, concourse, nauigation, trade, and populosity, very hardly giuing place to any one in *Europe*, doth absolutely excell all the Cities of the world for good gouernment, or at least doth match and equall them ; that very *London* so venerable for the antiquitie, so honorable for the customes, so profitable for life, noble in renowne, euen beyond the names both of our Countrey it selfe, and of our nation, the birth-place of *Constantine* the Great, and inmost recesse, or chamber of her Kings, that very City, that very *London* whether your locall parent, or louing foster mother, shall not grace, or honor you more, then you shall grace, and honor her, and *England* also.

VALETE.

From Sir WILLIAM SEGAR

Knight, GARTER, principall King
of Armes of ENGLAND, a fpeciall Letter
to the Author, concerning the prefent worke.

Sir:

 Haue viewed and re-
uiewed your book with
good deliberation, and
find, that you haue done
the office of a very wor-
thy Aduocate to plead fo
well for fo famous a Cli-
ent as the City of *London*
in her generality, which as I gratulate vnto her,
and to all intereffed parties, fo I fhall much more
gratulate to her, and you, the honour and vfe
of fo faire a labour, if I may once fee that publike: And for my part, confidering that you
define nothing, but lye onely vpon the defenfiue,
and affirmatiue, againft affaylers, and denyers,
with due fubmiffion for the iudiciall part to the
proper Court of Honor, the illuftrious high Mar-
fhalls of ENGLAND by Commiffion;

I see no caufe why your learned worke, may not receiue the glory of publike light, and that moft renowned Citie the benefit of honors encreafe, for incouragement of enriching enduftrie; And fo with my hearty refpects I reft,

Your very louing friend

WILLIAM SEGAR
Garter.

THE

THE TRVE COPIES OF
the Letters mentioned after
the Booke.

The firſt letter, from the Citizen in the behalfe
and cauſe of his eldeſt ſonne, to a ſpeciall
friend, of whoſe loue, and learning
he reſted confident.

Right Worthy Sir,

IF hauing beene at no ſmall charge, and ſome care, to breed my ſonne
vp in Gentleman like qualities, with purpoſe the rather to enable
him for the ſeruice of God, his Prince, and Countrey, I am very curious to remoue from him, as a Father, all occaſions, which might either
make him leſſe eſtemed of others, or abate the leaſt part of his edge; I ſay,
not towards the honeſty of life onely, but towards the ſplendor thereof,
and worſhip alſo, my hope is, that I ſhall not in your worthy iudgement,
ſeeme either inſolent, or vaine glorious.

Truth and Iuſtice are the onely motiues of my ſtirring at this preſent.
For, as I mortally hate that my Son ſhould beare himſelfe, aboue himſelf
ſo ſhould I diſclaime my part in him, if being vniuſtly ſought to be emba-
ſed, be ſillily loſt any inch of his due. He hath beene diſgraced as no Gentleman borne, when yet not hee but I his Father was the Apprentiſe,
thankes be to God for it. They cannot obiect to him want of faſhion, they
cannot obiect to him the common vices, badges rather of reprobates then
of Gentlemen: They cannot obiect to him cowardiſe, for it is well knowne
that he dares defend himſelfe: nor any thing elſe vnworthy of his name,
which is neither new, nor ignoble: But mee his poore father they obiect
vnto him, becauſe I was once an Apprentiſe.

Wiſe

Wife Sir Thomas Moore *teacheth vs, vnder the names, and perfons of his* Eutopians, *that victories, and atchieuements of wit are applauded, farre aboue thofe of forces: and feeing reuerence to God, & to our Prince, commandeth vs. (as his Maiefties booke of Duells doth affirme (not to take the office of iuftice from Magiftrates, by priuate rafh reuenges, I haue compelled my fonne, vpon Gods bleffing, and mine, to forbeare the fword till by my care he may be found not to be in the wrong. For if it be true,* that by Apprentifhip we forfeit our titles to natiue Generie: *God forbid that my fonne fhould vfurpe it. And if it be not true, then fhall he haue a iuft ground to defend himfelfe, and his aduerfaries fhall ftand conuicted of ignorance, if not of enuie alfo.*

Thefe are therefore very earneftly to pray you, to cleare this queftion. For, in the City of London *there are at this prefent many hundreds of Gentlemens children Apprentifes, infinite others haue beene, and infinite will be: and all the parts of* England *are full of families, either originally raifed to the dignity of Gentlemen out of this one moft famous place: or fo reftored, and enriched as may well feeme to amount to an originall raifing. And albeit I am very confident, that by hauing once beene an Apprentife in* London, *I haue not loft to be a Gentleman of birth, nor my fonne, yet fhall I euer wifh, and pray rather to refemble an heroicke* Walworth, *a noble* Philpot, *an happie* Capel, *that learned Sheriffe of* London *Mr.* Fabian, *or any other famous Worthies of this royall City, out of any whatfoeuer obfcureft parentage, then that being defcended of great Nobles, to fall by vice farre beneath the rancke of pooreft Prentifes.*

In requitall of your care in this point, you fhall fhortly receiue (if I can obtain my defire) out of the records & monuments of London, *a Roll of the names, and Armes of fuch principall friends as haue beene aduanced to Honor, and Worfhip, throughout the Realme of* England *from the degree of Citizens. A warrantable defigne, by the example of the Lord chiefe Iuftice* Cooke, *who hath beftowed vpon the world (in fome one or other of his bookes of reports) a fhort Catalogue of fuch as haue beene eminently beholding to the Common Lawes, and if I fhould faile in that, yet doe I promife you a lift or Alphabet of Apprentifes names, who by their enrollments will appeare vpon good Record, to haue beene fonnes of Gentlemen from all the parts of* England.

Neither

Neither let your approued vertue doubt, but that in the meane time you shall finde vs very ready to shew our free, and honest mindes, in all commendable, and disenuious emulations, with the best Gentlemen whosoeuer. Which disposition measure not by the few Angells you receiue in this Letter. For what are twenty in such a case?

If this my suite, and request, cary the lesse regard, because it comes but from a priuate Citizen, be pleased I pray to vnderstand, that in me, though being but one man, multitudes speake, and that out of a priuate pen, a publike cause propounds it selfe. And yet I come not single. For with this Letter of mine, I send you two other. The one from a worshipfull friend, and kinsman of mine, written to me, and the other of my Cousin his second sonne, much what of one nature with this of mine. And so with my loue, and best respects remembred, I commit you to Gods holy keeping, and rest, &c.

The true Copies of those two other Letters, whereof
in the former there is mention.

The Fathers Letter.

COusin, I pray peruse the enclosed, which troubleth me as much as it doth my sonne, and seeke satisfaction of such as are skilfull indeed. I care not for charge, for looke whatsoeuer it costs I will beare it. In the meane while comfort my childe, for if it bee so as hee writes, hee shall not stay in London, though it cost me fiue hundred Pounds. And so in great hast I leaue you to our Lord Christ, &c.

The

The Apprentifes Letter to his Father.

MOst deare, and most louing Father, my most humble dutie remembred vnto you. Thefe are to giue you to vnderftand, that
my body is in good health, praifed be God, but my minde, and fpirits are
not, for they are very much troubled. For, fo it is Sir, that albeit my
Mafter be a very worthy, and an honeft Citizen, and that my feife, doing as an Apprentife ought (which I doe willingly, not refufing any thing,
as remembring St. Peters precept, Serui, fubditi eftote in timore Do-
mini) am as well vfed in this houfe, as if I were with you; yet by rea-
ding certaine bookes, at fpare houres, and conferring with fome who take
vpon them to be very well skill'd in Heraldry, I am brought to beleeue,
that by being a Prentife, I lofe my birth right, and the right of my blood
both by father, and mother, which is to be a Gentlemen, which I had rather dye, then to endure. This is my griefe, and this the caufe why my
minde is fo troubled, as I cannot eat, nor fleepe in quiet: Teares hinder
me from writing more, and therefore moft humbly crauing pardon, and
your moft fathe ly bleffing, I commit you to God, &c.

From London, &c.

THE

THE
CITIES ADVOCATE,
In a queſtion of Honor,
and Armes.

Whether Apprentiſhip extinguiſheth
Gentrie.

The Contents of this firſt part.

1 *T*He *preſent queſtion very important for many great cau-*
ſes.Two Crowned Queenes of England *& much of the*
*Nobility parties to it.*Bullen *&* Calthorpe *L. Majors of*
London; *their intereſſes in royall blood. What* Quæſtio
ſtatus, *and what the leaſt* capitis diminutio *is. Only the*
baſe neglect it. Honour a faire Starre. Diſparagement
odious. *Preuention of miſchiefes by determining this*
queſtion. Proud Citie-races vnworthy of the Citie.

2 *The Cities Honors in* Armes *proued out of ancient Monu-*
ments. The L.Fitz Walter, *Standard-bearer of* London.
Claurie *and* Biallie *two termes in old blazon.*

3 *The tranſcendent power of opinion. To derogate from the*
ſplendor of birth, reputed a wrong. Whence comes the pre-
ſent queſtion of Apprentiſhip.

4 *The maine reason why some doe hold, that* Apprentiſhip extinguiſheth Gentrie. *Apprentiſhip no bondage either in truth, or at all. The caſe truely propounded. The skill of honeſt gettings a precious myſtery. What kinde of contract that ſeemes to be, which is betweene* Maſter *and* Apprentiſe.

5 *An objection that* Apprentiſhip *is a kinde of bondage. The fine folly of* Eraſmus *in his Etymologie of an* Apprentiſe. *The compariſon betweene* Seruus *among* Ciuilians, *and* Apprentiſes *among Engliſhmen, holds not. What the word* Apprentiſe *meanes.* Sir Thomas Smiths *error in confounding ſeruitude and diſcipline.*

6 7. 8. *Particular points touching* Seruus. Sanctuarie *at the Princes image.* Manumiſſion, *and Recaptiuitie by Law. None of thoſe points concerne* Apprentiſes *more then Souldiers, Schollers, or religious nouices.*

9. 10. *The finall cauſe denominates the action, and proues* Apprentiſhip *not to be baſe. The contrarie opinion pernicious to manners, and to good Commonweale among vs, chiefly now. The different face of both opinions in daily experience.*

The

The First Part.

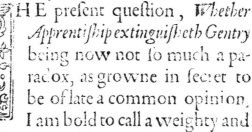

HE prefent queftion, *Whether Apprentiſhip extinguiſheth Gentry* being now not ſo much a paradox, as growne in ſecret to be of late a common opinion, I am bold to call a weighty and important queftion vniuftly grounded vpon the learned folly of *Eraſmus* of *Roterdam,* and the incircumſpection of Sir *Thomas Smith* Knight,in his booke *de Republica Anglorum,* and out of certaine wandring conceits hatcht among trees & tillage, as ſhall appeare hereafter. Weighty and important I am bold to call it,and it is ſo. Becauſe in looking out vpon the concernings of the caſe,I finde that proſpect ſo ſpacious,that within the compaſs thereof, as well the greater as the leſſer Nobilitie of *England* are very notably,and very inexplicably enwrapped. What doe I ſay of the ſubalternall Nobilitie,when the Royall name it ſelfe (with all humble reuerence be it ſpoken) was deeply intereſſed in the propoſition? For Queene *Elizabeth,* though a free Monarch,and chiefe of the Engliſh in her turne, was a party to the cauſe,which ſhee ingenuouſly, and openly acknowledged, calling Sir *Martin Calthorpe,* kinſman, (as indeed he was)

being

being at that time Knight, and Lord Maior of London: Yea Sir *Godfrey Bullen* (Knight also and Lord Maior of *London*) was lineall Anceſtor to Queene *Anne* her mother (ſaith *Camden* in his Annals) no longer before then in the reigne of *Henry* the ſixth King of *England.* Both which Knights(being alſo Gentlemen borne, & of right Worſhipfull Families) aſcended by due degrees from the condition of *Apprentiſes* to the greateſt annuall honor of this Kingdome. It is weighty and important, becauſe without much impropriety of ſpeech, it may be called *quæſtio ſtatus,* which in the ancient phraſe of the Emperour *Iuſtinian,* is as much to ſay as a tryall, whether one is to be adiudged bond, or free, ſeruile, or ingenuous, and implieth that odious, and vnnaturall ſequel, which by *Textuiſts* hath to name, *Capitis diminutio:* wherof though the Romane lawes make a threefold diuiſion, yet in this our queſtion, if but onely the third and loweſt degree were incurred, which hápneth, *cum qui ſui juris fuerunt, cœperunt alieno iuri ſubieĉti eſſe,* that alone ſhould keepe vs from neglect. It is weighty and important, and can appeare none other, becauſe it directly tends to darken, and as it were to intercloud the luminous body of that beauteous planet H O N O R, with not onely foule but laſting ſpots. For what

can

can lightly be a more difparagement, then for the
free to become a kind of bondmen, or to be come
of fuch? Nay, there is nothing without vs, which
can bee of fo great difparagement. Finally, it is
weighty, and important for very many other rea-
fons, and particularly becaufe it is not onely fit
that ftates of opinions fhould be rectified in this
kinde, as breeding bad affections among people
of the fame nation (from whence great mifchiefes
often rife, euen to hatred, quarrels, and homicides)
but that fuch alfo, as through vanity, or other fick-
neffe of the wit, or iudgement, difdaine to feeme
either Citie-borne, or Citie-bred, or to owe any
thing of their worfhip, or eftate, either to the City,
or to Citizens, may vnderftand their owne place,
and true condition, left they be conuinced to be a-
mong them, who are vnworthy of fo honeft either originall or acceffion as the Citie yeeldeth.

But let vs firft behold the Cities Honour in
Armes, as it ftands difplayed in ancient _Heraldry_,
and as it is commented vpon out of authenticke
Monuments in that worthily well commended
Survey of L o n d o n, compofed by that diligent
Chronologer, and vertuous Citizen M._Iohn Stowe_;
The prefent figure with the fame words as here
they ftand, is a copy of that which an old imper-
fect larger volume at the Office of Armes contai-
neth.   **There**

THE BADGES
OF LONDON

OF THE CITIE
OF LONDON
THE LORD
FITZ-WALTER
BANNERER

There needs no greater demonſtration of the Cities ancient honor, and of her peoples free qualitie, then this, that a principall Baron of the Realm of *England* was by tenure her Standard-bearer. The figure of St *Paul* (titularie patron of *London*) aduanced it ſelfe in the Standard, and vpon the ſhield thoſe famous well-knowne Armories of the Croſſe, and Weapon. The like picture of which Apoſtle was alſo embroidered in the caparifons of that horſe of warre, which for the purpoſe of the Cities ſeruice he receiued of gift at the hands of the Lord Maior. Vpon the Standard-bearers coat armour are painted the hereditarie enſignes of his owne illuſtrious Familie, that is to ſay, *Or, a Feſſe betweene two Cheuerns Gules.* Which kind of field the ancients called *Claurie*, perhaps *à clariate*, becauſe ſuch fields as were all of one colour made their charges the more clearely ſeene, and perſpicuous. And as they gaue to that ſpecies of blazon a peculiar name for the dignitie, ſo did they alſo aſſigne to this manner of bearing two *Cheuerns*, the terme *Biallie*, or a coat *Biallie, a numero binario.* In which braue times had that noble Gentleman, but ſlightly, and farre off ſuſpected, that he diſplayed that banner, for a kind of bondmen, or as for their ſeruice, his great heroick ſpirit

C   **would**

would rather haue trodden such an office vnder foot, In good assurance therefore of this common causes iustice, we proceed.

Sound opinion (meaning doctrine) is the anchor of the world, and opinion (meaning a worthy conceit of this or that person) is the principall ingredient which makes words, or actions relish well, and all the *Graces* are, without it, little worth. To take the same from any man that hee is a Gentleman-borne is a kind of disenablement, and preiudice, at leastwise among the weake (who consider no further then seemings) that is to say among almost all. Consequently a wrong. And if a wrong then due to be redressed. To find iniurie, we must first enquire

Whether Apprentiship extinguisheth Gentrie

4 The maine reason, certainly the most generall, vsed to proue, that it doth, is, *That Apprentiship is a kinde of bondage,* and bondage speciallie voluntarie (in which case the Imperiall law-rule, *non officit natalibus in seruitute fuisse,* may bee perhaps defectiue) extinguisheth natiue Gentrie. But I denie that *Apprentiship* is either *vera seruitus,* or *omnino seruitus.*

For explication of this difficultie, I will set before your eyes the case as it is. A Gentleman hath

a fonne, whom he meanes to breed vp in an Art
of thrift, not rifing meerely out of a ftocke of wit,
or learning, but out of a ftocke of money, and
credit, managed according to that Art; and for
this caufe hee brings his child at 15. or 16. yeares
old, more, or leffe, to the Citie of *London*, prouides
him a Mafter, and the youth, by his fathers coun-
cell, willing becomes an Apprentife, that is to fay,
interchangeably feales a written contract with
his Mafter by an indented inftrument. That he,
for his certaine yeares true and faithfull feruice,
fhall learne that precious myftery of how to
gaine honeftly, and to raife himfelfe. Let the legal
and ordinarie forme of that inftrument (extant in
Wefts Precedents, and familiar euery where) be du-
ly pondered, and it will appeare a meere ciuill
contract, which as all the world knowes, a bondman is vncapable of. If you would know vnder
what kinde, or fpecies of contract that doth fall.
I anfwer. That it feemes to be a contract of *per-
mutation*, or *interchange*: In which mutuall obligation, or conuention, the act of binding is no
more, but that (as reafon and iuftice would) the
Mafter might be determinately for the time, and
fufficiently for the manner, fure to enioy his Apprentife. Apprètifhip being therfore, but an effect

of

of a ciuill contract, occafioned, and caufed by that
prudent refpect which the Contrahents mutually
haue to their lawfull and honeft commodity, and
fuch onely as are free-borne , being capable to
make this contract with effect, *Apprentiſhip doth
not extinguiſh Gentry.*

On the contrarie, it is vrged : That although
Apprentiſhip bee not a true bondage to all con-
ftructions, and purpofes, yet, that it is a temporary
bondage, and equall (for the time it lafteth) to
very feruitude. In which opinion *Erafmus* is, making his Etymologie of our Prentifes to be , for
that they are like to fuch as are bought with money, *pares emptitijs,* which conceipt, as it is more li-
terate, then happie, fo, if it were fet to fale, would
find fevv Chapmen, but to laugh at it. For *Erafmus*
is afwell proued to be *errans mus in obfcurorum vi-
rorum Epiſtolis,* as Apprentifes in *England* to be *pares emptitijs.* But vve abfolutely deny that Apprentiſhip is in any fort a kinde of bondage. For not-
withftanding that to proue it be fo, they make a
parallel betvveen the ancient *Roman* feruitude, and
the *London* apprentiſhip, yet will thefe *comparata,*
be found *diſparata,* if not *diſparatiſsma.* For *feruus*
among the old Romans, was fo called of *feruando*
of preferuing or fauing, and not of *feruiendo,* of
seruing,

feruing, faith the Law-maker himfelfe, the Emperor *Iuftinian.* But the word *Apprentife* commeth of *Aprenti,* the French word, a raw fouldier, or young learner, *Tyro, rudis difcipulus;* or of the *French* verbe, which fignifies to learne, or of the *Latine* word *apprehendo,* or *apprendo,* which properly is to lay hold of, and tranflatiuely to learne, which deriuations are confonant to the thing, and true howfoeuer Sir *Thomas Smith* in his bookes *de Republica Anglorum,* not remembring to diftinguifh betweene feruitude and difcipline, bondage, and regular breeding, iniurioufly defined them to be a kind of bondmen (meaning meere flaues, and not as in fome places of *England,* bondfmen are taken for fuch as are in bonds for actionable caufes) and fuch bondmen as differ onely thus from very bondmen (whofe like words for fignification are thofe fouleft ones, *flaues* and *villaines*) that Apprentifes be but for a time certaine. An ouerfight which I could haue wifhed far off from fo graue and learned a Gentleman, as that Knight, who was of priuy Counfell, in the place of Secretarie, to Queene *Elizabeth.*

Againe, that which did conftitute a bondman among the old *Romans,* was fuch a power and right, vefted in the Lord, ouer the very body of his

C 3 bond-

bondman, or flaue, as defcending to him vnder
some receiued title, or other *iure gentium*, was
maintained to him, *iure ciuili Romanorum*. By vertue whereof he became proprietarie in the perfon
of his bondman, as in the body of his oxe, horfe,
or any other beaft he had, which proprietarifhip
was indeterminable, but only by *manumiffion*, and
that act meerely depended vpon the will of his
Lord, without any endentment, or condition on
behalfe of the flaue, which a right Roman would
neuer endure to heare of from his bondman. Finally (which in the qualitie of that feruitude was
moft bafe,) *feruus* among them, *nullum caput ha-
buit*, had no head in law, and neither was *in cen-
fu*, nor *in luftro condito*; afmuch to fay, that they
were out of the number of men, their names being neither put, as among fuch as had wherewith
to pay in the Rolles of their Exchequer, or tables
of their *Capitol*, nor, as bodies wherewith to ferue
in the generall mufters of their Commonweale,
but (to bee briefe) were reputed *ciuilitèr mortui*,
dead in Law, death, and bondage being alike a-
mong them, without any more reputation of being members in the body politique, then brute
cattell, for bondmen were reputed no body, *ferui
pro nullis habiti*.

                                  And

And albeit the authority of the commonweale vpon this good ground of State, *intereſt reipublicæ ne quis re ſua male ʊtatur,* and the Maieſtie of Soueraigne Princes, meerly as in honor, and as moued with commiſeration of humane miſeries, did ſometime interpoſe it ſelfe vpon iuſt cauſes; as, where the Lord did immeaſurably tyranniſe, or the bondman tooke Sanctuary at the Emperours ſtatue, and image, or, at the altar of ſome one or other of their gods (an example whereof is in *Plautus*) yet the bondman after manumiſſion, continued in ſuch relation to his late Lord that in certaine caſes, (as ingratitude) he who was once enfranchiſed was adiudged backe to his patron, and condemned againe to a farre more miſerable ſeruitude then euer.

Theſe things conſidered, and nothing being like in Apprentiſhip, who liues ſo careleſſe of the honour of the Engliſh name, as to bring the diſciples of honeſt Arts, and Schollers of myſteryes in ciuill trade, and commerce for vertuous cauſes, all called by the faire title of Apprentiſes, into the ſtate or qualitie of bondmen? Faire I call it, becauſe that title is common to them with the Inns of Court, where Apprentiſes at Law, are not the meaneſt Gentlemen. Apprentiſhip therefore is no voluntarie bondage, becauſe it is no bondage at all, but a

title

title onely of politicke or ciuill difcipline. Apprentifhip therefore doth not extinguifh Gentry. So then, Apprentifes, whether Gentlemen of birth or others, whatfoeuer their Indentures doe purport, and howfoeuer they feeme conditionall feruäts, are in truth not boûd to do, or to fuffer things more grieuous then yong fouldiers in armies, or fchollers in rigorous fchooles, or nouices in nouicefhips: each of whom in their kind vfually do, and fuffer things as bafe and vile in their owne quality, fimply, & in themfelues confidered, without refpect to the finall fcope, or aime of the firft inftitution, as perhaps the very meaneft of fiue thoufand Apprentifes in *London.*

The finall caufe therefore of euery ordination qualifies the courfe, and the end denominates the meanes and actions tending to it. For if that be noble, no worke is bafe prefcribed *in ordine*, or as in the way to that end. Though abftracting frô that confideration, the worke wrought, in the proper nature of it, be feruile. As, for a fouldier to dig or carie earth to a rampire, or for a ftudent to goe bare-headed to a fellow of the houfe within the Colledge, as far off as he can fee him, omitting the more deformed neceffitie, of fuffering priuate, or publike difciplines: or for a nouice in a nouicefhip to wafh difhes, or the like feeming-bafe workes, as by report, is vſuall. If then the generall ſcope, or finall reaſon of Apprentiſhip be honeſt, and worthy of a Gentlemã (as will appeare hereafter that it is) what can be clearer then that *Apprentiſhip* doth not extinguiſh *Gentry?*

I am the more feruent in this caſe; becauſe this one falſe conceit (at all times hurtful, but chiefly in theſe latter times, in which the meanes of eaſie maintenance are infinitely ſtraitned) that *for a Gentleman borne, or one that would aſpire to bee a Gentleman, for him to be an Apprentiſe to a Citizen, or Burgenſis, is a thing vnbeſeeming him,* hath fill'd our *England* with more vices, and ſacrificed more ſeruiceable bodies to odious ends, and more ſoules to ſinfull life, then perhaps any *one other vnciuill opinion* whatſoeuer. For they who hold it better to rob by land, or ſea, then to beg, or labour, doe daily ſee, and feele, that out of Apprentiſes riſe ſuch, as ſit vpon them, ſtanding out for their liues as malefactors, when they (a ſhame, and ſorrow to their kinred) vndergoe a fortune too vnworthy, euen of the baſeſt, of honeſt bondmen.

D   THE

The Contents of this second part.

The

The Second Part.

1 Hefe things confidered, how fhould it fall into the minde of any good, or wife difcouler, *That Apprentifes are a kind of bondmen,* and confequently, *That Apprentifhip extinguifheth natiue Gentry, and difenableth to acquifitiue?* For, if that opinion bee not guilty of impiety to our Mother Countrey, where that laudable policie of Apprentifhip neceffary for our nation, is exercifed as a point of feuere difcipline, warrantable in *Chriftianitie*; certainly it hath in it a great deale of iniurious temeritie, and inconfiderance; and why not impietie alfo, if they wilfully wrong the wifdome of *England,* their naturall common parent, whofe children are freeborne? Surelie, notorious inconfiderance is apparent, becaufe there are but two maine pillars of Common-weale, PRÆMIVM & PÆNA, *Reward* and *Punifhment.* Of which, in ciuill rewards, *Honor* is higheft, according to that of the moft eloquent *Tullie* in his perifhed workes, *de republica,* (as S. *Auguftine* citeth them) as that thing with which *bee would his Prince fhould bee fed and*

D 2 *nourifhed;*

nourished; and in his Philofophie hath vttered that
famous fentence concerning the fame, *Honos alit
artes, omnefq; accenduntur ad ftudia gloria.* Among
vs therefore coats of Armes , and titles of Gentlemen (which point the Knight beforefaid, howfoeuer erring in Apprentiles eftate , hath truely
noted to be commodious for the Prince) being
the moft familiar part of *Honor*, they rip vp, and
ouerturne the principall of thofe two pillars of
common-weale,frō the very bafis. A ftrange ouerfight, fpecially of profeffors of skill in the Arts of
publike gouernment, vnleffe perhaps they fpeake
it becaufe they would haue things reformed , or
changed in this particular of Apprentifhip.   But
we do not remember, that either Sir *Thomas Eliot*
in his Gouernor, or Sir *Thomas Chaloner,* (Leigier
Ambaffador for Queen *Elizabeth* in *Spaine*) in his
bookes of Latine Hexameters *de rep. Anglorum in-
ftaurandâ,* (publifhed with the verfes of the Lord
Treafurer *Burghley's* before it) or any other Author rightly vnderftanding our *England*, and her
generous people, did euer once taxe our Countries
policie in this point.   Yea, fome make it a *quære,*
whether the Cities difcipline had not more need
to be reduced neerer to the ancient feuerity thereof, confidering with what vices *London* flowes,
                                        and

and ouerflowes, then that it should bee abduced, though but a little, from it.

Now then let any one but rightly weigh with what confcience, or common fenfe, the firft inftitutors, or propagators of the Englifh forme of gouernment could lay vpon *Induftry,* and ciuill *Vertue* (whofe fubiect are the lawfull things of this life, and whofe neereft obiect is honor , and honeft wealth) fo foule a note as the brand of bondage, or any the leaft difparagement at all? whereas to quicken, & inflame affections in that kind, all wife Mafters in the moft noble ciuill Art gouernement, and all founders of Empire, and States, haue bent their counfels, and courfes, to cherifh fuch as are vertuoufly induftrious, yea, God himfelfe, (the onely beft patterne of gouernours) hath made it knowne, that euen Mechanicall qualities are his fpeciall gifts, and his infufed, as it were *charifmata.*

3 For *Mofes* hauing put into eternall monuments, that *Iabel* was *pater paftorum* (the moft an-Art of encreefe) and that *Iubal* was *pater canentium* (the firft of which inuentions was for neceffary prouifions of food, and raiment, & the fecond to glorifie God, and honeftly to folace men, towards fweetning the bitter curfe which *Adam*

D 3   drew

drew vpon humane life,) it is thirdly vnder added
in accomplifhment of the three maine heads to
which mortalls vfe to refer all their worldly ende-
uors (neceffitie,profit,& pleafure) that *Tubal Cain*
was *Malleator,* and *faber ferrarius,* an hammer-
Smith,or worker in yron, that being one of thofe
Arch-myfteries,*fine quibus non ædificatur ciuitas,* as
the words are in *Ecclefiafticus,* Nay, there belon-
ged in Gods owne iudgement fo great praife to
the particular excellency of fome artificers,as that,
in the building of *Salomons* Temple, they are regi-
ftred to all pofterities in Scripture; and their skill
is not onely made immortally famous,but a more
curious mention is put downe of their parentage,
and birth place, then of many great Princes,as in
Hirams cafe,not he the King,but the brafe-foun-
der. And in the new Teftament,*S.Paul,* being a
Gentlemen borne of a noble familie, a: the Ancients write) had the manuall Art of *Scænopœa,*commonly englifhed,Tent-making : vpon wch place
of St. *Pauls* trade (whereof in his Epiftles he doth
often glorie) it is declared to vs out of the *Rab-
bins,* that S. *Paul* (who himfelfe tells King *Agrippa*
that he had liued a *Pharifee;* according to the moft
certaine way of *Iewifm*) was brought vp fo, by a
traditionall precept, binding fuch a would ftudie
facred

facred letters, to learne fome one or other myfterie
in the Mechanicks. And at this prefent among
other things which the Turks retaine of the *Iewifh*
rites, this feemes one, when euen the *Sultan* himfelfe, or *Grand Signior* (as all his progenitors) is faid
to exercife a manuall trade, little, or much, commonly once a day. And in frefh memorie *Rodul-
phus* the Emperour had fingular skill in making
Dials, Watches, and the like fine works of Smith-
craft, as alfo a late great *Baron* of *England*, which
they practifed.

    4 If then fuch honor be done by God (as be-
forefaid) not onely to thofe which are neceffarie
handy-crafts, but to thofe alfo which are but the
handmaids of magnificence, and outward fplendor, as engrauers, founders, and the like; hee fhall
be very hardie who fhall embafe honeft *Induftry*
with difgracefull cenfures; and too vniuft, who
fhall not cherifh, or encourage it with praife and
worfhip, as the ancient excellent policie of *England* did, and doth, in conftituting corporations,
& adorning Companies with banners of Armes
and fpeciall men with notes of Nobleffe.

    5 And, as of all commendable Arts all wor-
thy Common-weales haue their vfe, fo, in *London*
they haue as it were their palace. But into the bodie

die of the Citie none generally are encorporated,
but such onely as through the strait gates of
Apprentiship aspire to the dignitie and state of
Citizens. That *Hebrew* bondmen were not, in
M o s e s law, among themselues, like to our
Apprentises (howsoeuer the seuenth yeare agrees
in time with the ordinarie time of our Apprentises obligation) is euident both in the bookes of
Exodus, and *Deuteronomie.* For, first, their title to
their bondmen grew to their Lords by a contract of bargaine, and sale, which was indeed a
kind of seruitude. For, when the seuenth yeare, in
which the bondage was to determine, and ex-
pire, if then he resolued not to continue a bondman for euer, he was compelled to leaue his wife
(if maried in his Lords house during bódage) together with his children, borne in that mariage
behinde him, though himselfe departed free, but
withall rewarded also. So that voluntarie bondage is not onely *de iure gentium* (as the *Romane*
lawes import, by which a man might sell himselfe, *ad participandum precium*) but also *de iure diui-
no positiuo.* By which notwithstanding it doth
not appeare, that such a bondage was any disparagement, or disenablement in *Iewish* blood a-
mong the *Iewes,* because in *Exodus* wee read of a
prouision

prouifion made for the *Hebrew* bond-woman, whom her Lord might take in mariage to himfelfe, or beftow her vpon his fon, if he fo thought good, but might not violate her chaftitie, as if hee had *ius in corpus.* But the condition of an Apprentife of *London* refembleth the condition of no perfons eftate in either of the lawes, *Diuine* or *Imperiall*; For he directly contracteth with his Mafter to learne his myfterie, or Art of honeft liuing, neither hath his Mafter (who therefore is but a Mafter, & not a Lord) *Defpoticũ imperium* ouer his Apprentife (that is, fuch a power as a Lord hath ouer flaue) but *quafi curaturam*, or a *Guardianfhip*, and is in very truth a meere *Difcipliner*, or Teacher, with authority of vfing moderate correction as a Father, not as a Tyrant, or otherwife. Immoderate correction whofoeuer doth vfe, is (by a gracious ftatute of the fifth of Queene *Elizabeth*) fubiect to be punifhed with the loffe of the Apprentife, by abfolutely taking him away.

6 Which things, fo often as I deeply ponder, I cannot but hold it as loofe, and as wandring a conceit, and as vnciuill a propofition in ciuill matters as any : *That Apprentifhip fhould be imagined either to extinguifh, or to extenuate the right of natiue Gentrie, or to difable any worthy, or fit perfon to acquifi-*

E   *tiue*

tiue Armories. For how can it in Gods name worke that effect, vnleſſe it be criminall to be an Apprentiſe? Becauſe no man loſeth his right to beare Armes, or to write Gentleman, vnleſſe hee be attainted in Law for ſuch a cauſe, the conuiction whereof doth immediately procure corruption in blood, which as in this caſe no man yet hath dreamed of.

Againe, when by the old common Law of *England* there are onely two ſorts of bondmen, that is to ſay, *villaines in groſſe,* and *villaines regardant to a Mannour,* and it is moſt certaine, that our *Apprentiſe,* or Schollar in Citie-myſteries, is neither one nor other of them, what ignorance then, or offence was mother at firſt of this, not paradox, but palpable abſurditie, that *Apprentiſhip extinguiſheth Gentry,* or that Apprentiſes are as with vs a kind of bondmen?

The

The Contents of this third part.

*E*2   *The*

The third Part.

1 Hough in the premiſſes wee ſeeme to our ſelues, to haue ſaid enough for eſtabliſhing our *Negation* in this importāt queſtion, that is to ſay, *That Apprentiſhip is not a kinde of bondage*, conſequently, that it cannot worke any ſuch effects as is before ſuppoſed, yet to leaue no tollerable curioſitie vnſatisfied, wee will ſet before vs, as in a table, the whole condition of an Apprentiſe. Meaning chiefly ſuch an *Apprentiſe* as being the ſon of a *Gentleman,* is bound to a Maſter, who exerciſeth the worthier Arts of Citizens, as Merchants by ſea, Aſſurers, Whole-ſale-men, & ſome ſuch few others which may more ſpecially ſtand in the firſt claſſe of the moſt generous myſteries, as thoſe in which the wit or minde hath a farre greater part then bodily labour.

2 Such an Apprentiſe therefore when firſt he comes to his Maſter is commonly but of thoſe yeares which are euery where ſubiect to correction. His ordinarie ſeruices theſe. Hee goes bareheaded, ſtands bare-headed, waytes bare-headed,

before

before his Mafter and Miftreffe,and,while as yet
he is the yongeft *Apprentife,* hee doth perhaps (for
difcipline fake) make old leather ouer-night
fhine with blacking for the morning, brufheth a
garment,runs of errands,keeps filence till he haue
leaue to fpeake, followes his Mafter, or vfhereth
his *Miftreffe,* and fometime my young *Miftreffes*
their daughters (among whom fome one, or
other of them doth not rarely proue the *Apprentifes* wife) walkes not farre out but with permif-
fion,and now, and then (as offences happen) he
may chance to be terribly chidden, or menaced,
or (which fometime muft be) worthily correc-
ted; though all this but onely *in ordine,* and in the
way to *Mafterfhip,* or to the eftate of a Citizen,
which laft worft part of this *Apprentifes* condition continues peraduenture for a yeare, or two,
and while hee is commonly but at the age of a
boy, or at the moft but of a lad,or ftripling. And,
take things at the very worft,hee doth nothing as
an *Apprentife* vnder his Mafter, which, when
himfelfe comes to be a Mafter his *Apprentifes* fhal
not doe,or fuffer vnder him.Such or the like is the
bittereft part of an *Apprentifes* happy eftate in this
world, being honeftly prouided, at his *Mafters*
charge of all things neceffarie,and decent. The

E 3 *Mafter*

Mafter in the meane-while feruing his *Apprentifes*
turne with inftruction, and vniuerfall conforma-
tion, or moulding of him to his Art, as the *Ap-*
prentife ferues his *Mafters* turne with obedience,
faith,and induftrie.

3 Here haue we a reprefentation of an *Ap-*
prentifes being,or rather the well-being of a child
vnder his father, who hath right of correction.
Vpon view whereof we demand, why it fhould
be fuppofed *That Apprentifhip extinguifheth Gentry?*
For if an Apprentife in *London* (fince to haue Apprentifes is a power not deriued to corporations
out of prerogatiue,and royall priuiledge, but out
of common Law) bee in their conceipts a kinde
of bondman, it muft either be, *ratione generis ob-*
fequij, or *ratione temporis adiecti,* or *contractus,* or
conditionis, or for all together; a fifth caufe being
hard to be either affigned,or imagined.

For the firft point (wch is in regard of the kind
of feruice)that is but an effect of the contract, or
bargaine,and confequently depends thereon, or
participates in nature with it; which not impor-
ting any kind of bondage,neither can the feruice
it felfe, due by that agreement, bee the feruice of a
bondman. So that as on the one fide wee grant,
that Apprentifes,as Apprentifes,doe fome things,
                                            which

which Gentlemen would not doe, that liued *ſui iuris*, ſpecially vpon a neceſſity to obey, yet on the other ſide we conſtantly deny, that they doe any of them, either as ſeruile, or as ſeruilely, but *propter finem nobilem*, that is, to learne an honeſt myſterie to enable them for the ſeruice of God and their Countrey, in the ſtation, place, or calling of a Citizen.

For the ſecond (which is in reſpect of a cer-taine time (as of ſeuen yeeres at leaſt) added and limited in the contract, that is meerely but a cir-cumſtance of the agreement, and *per conſequens* cannot alter the ſubſtance of the queſtion. For if Apprentiſes are not a kind of bondmen, abſtract-ing from the time which they are bound to ſerue, the addition of time, addeth nothing to the qua-lity of the contract, to make it ſeruile.

For the third (which is in regard of the con-tract, as it raiſeth a relation, or the titles betweene two, of Maſter, and ſeruant) if the very act of binding to performance, be a ſufficient reaſon to make Apprentiſes a kinde of bondmen, and ſo to diſenable them to Gentry, either deriuatiue, or ac-quiſitiue, the Maſters themſelues are alſo a kinde of bondmen, becauſe, *ſuo genere* they aſwell are bound as the Apprentiſes.

For

For the fourth (which is in refpect of the condition either vocally expreft, or vertually implide
in the contract) there is in it no proofe of bondage, but the contrarie. For in that the obligation is mutuall, it proues the Apprentife free as from
bondage, though (for the *Apprentifes* owne good)
not free from fubiection to difcipline. Becaufe
onely free men can make contracts, and challenge
the benefit of them. The verbe, not, *feruire*, but
the verbe, *deferuire* (which is of farre leffe weight)
comprifed in the inftrument, or Indenture, and
containing the whole force of the obligation,
hath onely in that place the fenfe of *obfequi, & fa-
cere,* to obey, and doe as an *Apprentife,* and not according to the ancient fenfe, which it had among
the *Romanes.* This ought not to feeme a paradox. For the word *dominari,* to which *feruire*
is a relatiue, and the word *dominus,* haue in tract of
time beene fo foftened, and familiarifed, as they
are growne to be words of fingular humanity.
And what fo common among the noble as to
profeffe to ferue? But the relation conftituted in
this cafe, is peculiar, and proper, the odious word
dominus is not there at all, nor *feruus,* no nor *famu-
lus;* the relation conftituted is directly named betweene Mafter, and Apprentife : a cleare cafe that
                                                        all

all iniuries to blood, and nature, are of purpose a-
uoided in thofe conuentions; and *conuentiones* they
are called in the interchangeably fealed inftrument it felfe. So cleare a cafe, that in the Oath
which all freemen make in the Chamber of *London* at their firft admiffion, this claufe among many others, is fworne vnto by them, That they fhall
take *None* Apprentife, but if he be *Free borne,* that
is to fay, no *Bond-mans* fonne : which are the very
words of the oath. Thus carefully open was the
eye of inftitution in this noble point of the Cities
policy, to preuent that no ftaine, no blemifh, nor
indignitie fhould wrong the fplendor thereof.
A thing which could not but follow ineuitably,
if they who prouided againft admiffion of *bond-
mens* iffue, into the eftate of apprentifhip, fhould
themfelues by making apprentifes, make bondmen; or fhould in any fort embafe their blood,
whofe Mafters they were to be, as to the purpofe
of comming to bee Citizens in time. They neuer
meant to make any man bond, who would haue
none but the fonnes of free-borne perfons bound
apprentifes. It fhall be wilfull ignorance or ma-
lice from hence forth to maintaine the contrary.

4 A moft memorable exáple in Scripture to the
purpofe of the prefent queftion is that of *Iacob* and

F *Laban,*

Laban in the nine and twentieth Chapter of *Ge-nesis*, where the time (*seuen yeares*) yea, & the very word (*seruire*) are plaine in that contract which was made betweene the vncle, and the nephew: yet who did euer say that *Iacob* was for this a kind of bondman? The reason why he was not, riseth from consideration of the finall cause, or intention of the contract, which is recorded to haue beene honorable; the obtaining of a worthy wife, and of an estate to maintaine her with. Neither, when he was no longer defrauded of *Rahel* then seuen daies after his first seuen yeares, and when in the fruition of *Rahel* he serued also other seuen yeares, was he a kind of bondman, by as it were a relapse, or as by a cessation of expecting his reward, which he enioyed in enioying her. Out of which it followeth, that as *Iacob* was no kind of bondman though he serued, and serued out all his time twice ouer, so neither are Apprentises. And from this place of the Bible it is vnanswerablie proued that bodily seruice, is a laudable meanes to atchieue any good, or honorable purpose; a meanes truly worthy of a Gentleman.

5 Hereunto we finally adde, and repeat, that as an Apprentise tyes himselfe to his Master in the word *deseruire*, that is, *to obey*, and doe, restrictiuely

to

to the ancient reafon , and traditionall difcipline
of Apprentifhip in *London,* fo the Mafter tyes himfelfe to his Apprentife in the word *docere,* in lieu
of his honeft feruice, to teach him his Art to the
vtmoft. Which Mafters part is growne to fuch
eftimation as that Apprentifes now come commonly like wiues with portions to their Mafters.
If then Apprentifhip be a kinde of feruitude, it is
either a pleafing bondage, or a ftrange madneffe
to purchafe it with money.

   6 An Apprentife therefore, as an Apprentife,
being neither *ratione obfequij, temporis, contraƈus,*
nor *conditionis* in any kinde a bondman , is in no
refpeƈt a bondman : and hath therefore no more
loft his title, and right to *Gentrie,* then hee hath
done to any goods, chattels, lands, royalties, or
any thing elfe, which, if hee had neuer beene an
Apprentife, either had, might, or ought to haue
come vnto him. Nay, much leffe can Gentry bee
loft in this cafe, then right to lands, and goods,
how much more inherent the rights of blood are
then the rights of fortune. For, according to the
law-rule, *iura fanguinum nullo iure ciuili dirimi pof-*
funt; whereas thofe other may be diffolued. And,
that *Gentry* is a right of blood may appeare by
this, that no man can truely alienate the fame, or
veft

vest another in it,though legally he may,in case of Adoption, which is but an humane inuention in imitation of nature, and therefore *in rei veritate*, no alienation at all, but a fiction, or an acception in law as if it were such.　So that none can any more passe away his gentrie, to make another a Gentleman thereby, who was not a Gentleman before, then he can passe away any habit, or quality of the minde, as vertue, or learning, to make another honest, or learned, who was vnlearned, or dishonest before.　For Gentry is a quality of blood,or name,as vertue, and learning are of the minde.　Vpon which reason that rule of law is grounded, which teacheth vs, that *annulus signatorius ornamenti appellatione non continetur.*

7　To all this if it bee replied :　That Apprentiship is a kind of bondage, for that if an Apprentise abandon his Masters seruice; his Master may both fetch him backe, as Lord for the time ouer his seruants body, and compell him also to liue vnder obedience. We answer thus. That such a power ouer the bodie of an Apprentise is not sufficient to constitute a bondman, though the seruice of the Apprentise belongs to the Master, Gods part in him,and the Commonweales being first deducted.

Aristotle

Ariſtotle held, that onely the *Grecians* were free, and all the barbarou̅, that is to ſay, all not *Grecians*, were bond. Some among vs ſeeme *Ariſtotelians* in this point, who as he glorioufly ouer-valued his Country-men, ſo theſe ouer-value their paragon-Gentry, and repute none worthie of Armes, and Honor but themſelues, we ſuppoſing on their behalfe, that they are indeed not vaine-pretenders onely, but true deſcendents from the moſt vnqueſtionable noble races, howſoeuer troubled perhaps with ſome little of the ſpirit of vanitie, and of too too much ſcorne of others. But as the *Italians* in our time, notwithſtanding they thinke meanely of all who are not *Italians*, calling them (in *Ariſtotles* humor) *Tramoutani*, and in that word implying them to be barbarous, doe commit an error, aſwell as that great Philoſopher, ſo thoſe Gentlemen (how eminently noble ſoeuer) will be likewiſe found to liue in errour, for that others alſo may bee truely Gentlemen, for any thing which as yet is ſpoken in the former Sophiſme: *videlicet; The Maſter hath power ouer his Apprentiſes bodie :* Ergo, *Apprentiſes are a kinde of bondmen.* Becauſe if ſuch a power bee enough to conſtitute a bondman, wee will ſay nothing of thoſe free-borne perſons being in minoritie,

whoſe

whofe bodies their *Guardians,*may not onely by a
right in law, fetch backe after efcape, or flight,
but giue away alfo in mariage. Nay, if for that reafon Apprentifes, borne Gentlemen, fhall bee
thought to haue forfeited their *Gentry,* in what
eftate are all the fonnes, and children of good
houfes in *England,* whofe bodies their parents by
a right of nature,may fetch back after flight,& exercife their pleafure, or difpleafure vpon thē, euen
to difinherifon ? Nay, in what cafe are fouldiers
(to whom moft properly,and moft immediately
the Honor of Armes doth belong) who for
withdrawing themfelues from their banner, or
Captaine without leaue, may not only be forced
backe to ferue, but (according to the vfuall difcipline of warre) may by martiall Law bee han-
ged vp,or fhot at the next tree,or wherefoeuer,de-
priued of breath at once,and of braue reputation
together ? So abfurd it is to difpute, that the power of a Mafter,by the title of a contract ouer the
body of an Apprentife, in cafe of difcipline, doth
conuince a feruilitie of condition in the fufferer.
For if the right to exercife corporall coerction
fhould abfolutely conftitute a ftate of bondage in
the fubiect, the iniurie of that vntrue affertion
would reach to perfons of farre higher marke
then

then City-prentifes, as is moft plainely proued.
And therefore they muft alledge fomewhat elfe
befides fubiection of bodie to draw the eftate of
Apprentifhip into that degree of reproach, which
as they cannot doe, wee hauing preuented thofe
obiections, fo muft they leaue it cleare from taint,
or fcandall.

8 We lay it downe therefore out of all the an-
tecedences for a cleare conclufion : That Apprentifes are fo farre from being a kinde of bondmen, as that in our Common-weale they then
firft begin *habere caput*, and to be *aliqui*: to bee of
account, and fome bodie.   For Apprentifhip in
London is a degree, or order of good regular fub-
iects, out of whofe as it were Nouicefhips, or
Colledges, Citizens are fupplied.   Wee call them
Colledges according to the old *Romane* Law-
phrafe, or fellowfhips of men, for fo indeed they
are, comprehended within feuerall corporations,
or bodies of free perfons, intended to bee confo-
ciated for commerce, according to confcience,
and iuftice, and named *Companies*, each of them fe-
uerally bearing the title of their feuerall worthy
Monopolies, as Drapers, Salters, Clothworkers,
and fo forth.   Wee fay as before, that *Apprentifes*
in the reputation of our Commonweale, when
firft

firſt they come to bee *Apprentiſes* then firſt begin to be ſome bodie, and that Apprentiſhip is a degree, to which out of youth, and yong men, who haue no vocation in the world, they are aduanced and that out of Apprentiſes, by other aſcents or ſteps, as *donari ciuitate*, to come to bee free of *London*, or Citizens, from thence to be of their companies Liuerie, the gouernours of Companies, as *Wardens*, and *Maſters*, and gouernors in the City, as Common-counſel-men, Aldermens-deputies, Sheriffes, and Aldermen; and laſtly the principall gouernour, or head of the Citie, the Lord Maior; yea ſometimes alſo Counſellors of Eſtate to the Prince (whereof Maſter *Stowe* hath examples) are very orderly elected; and the whole policie diſpoſed after as excellent a forme as moſt at this day vnder heauen.

9 True it is, that Apprentiſhip, as it is a degree, ſo is it the loweſt degree, or claſſe of men in *London.* Loweſt wee ſay, that it may come to the higheſt, according to that of S. *Auguſtine*, and of common ſenſe, that thoſe buildings riſe higheſt, and ſtand faſteth, whoſe foundations are deepeſt. And as Apprentipiſh is the firſt in order, & meaneſt in dignity, ſo can that be no title to embaſe the vocation, becauſe there muſt be a firſt in all things.

Of

Of this degree the flat round Cap, haire clofe-cut,
narrow falling-band, courfe fide-coat, clofe-hofe,
cloath ftockings, and the reft of that feuere habite
was in antiquitie, not more for thrift, and vfeful-
neffe, then for diftinction, and grace, and were o-
riginally arguments, or tokens of vocation, or calling, which point of ancient difcipline the *Catoes*
of *England,* graue common Lawyers, to their high
commendation therein, retaine in their profeffion, and profeffors at this prefent, euen to the par-
tie-coulored coates of feruing men at *Serieants*
Feafts. An obiect, far more ridiculous among the
new-fhapes of our time (enemie of rigour, and
difcipline) then that of *Apprentifes* At which retained fignes, and diftinctiue notes among Lawyers, though younglings, and friuolous nouices,
may fomewhat wonder, till the caufe be vnder-
ftood, yet is the thing it felfe fo farre in it felfe from
deferuing contempt, as that they who fhould offer it, would themfelues bee laughed at. For the
late Lord *Coke,* in the preface of his third booke
of *Reports,* hath affirmed for the dignitie of the
word *Apprentife,* that an *Apprentife* at Law is a
double reader, whofe degree is next to that of a
Serieant at Law, who is only inferiour to a Iudge,
and to no other degree of Lawyers.

G   Here

10 Here now let me be bold to fay, that *Apprentifes* feeme to haue drunke and facrificed too deepely to their new Goddeffe, Saint *Fafhion.* An Idoll which was alwayes noted fatall to the *Englifh.* As at the periods, or vniuerfall concuffions of Empire in our portion of great *Britaine,* may in old Writers bee obferued. This they doe not without wrong in our opinions to the honeftie of their degree, at leaftwife in fo farre abandoning their proper ornament, the *Cap* (anciently a note of libertie among the *Romans*) as not to haue one day at leaft in the yeare, wherein to celebrate the feaft of their *Apprentifhip* in the peculiar garbe thereof, which they fhould doe well and wifely to frequent for downe-bearing of contumelie, and fcorne, by making profeffion in this wife, that they glorie in the enfignes of their honeft calling.

11 For reuocation of which into vfe though we fee no manner of hope, yet are thofe late Magiftrates of the Citie who laboured to reduce Apprentifhip to practife this laudable point of outward conformitie, not the leffe to bee commended: and it were to be wifhed perhaps, that inftead of fcattering Libels, and of difcouering inclinations to tumult, Apprentifes had rather fubmit-

mitted their vnderſtandings, and reſigned their
wills in this particular to their louing ſuperiours,
making humble, and wiſe obedience the glorie of
their perſons, much rather then apparell in
the faſhion. For they who are not aſhamed of
their profeſſion, ought not to be aſhamed of the
enſignes, and tokens of their profeſſion, or degree.
They indeed are out of faſhion who are not in
that faſhion which is proper to their qualitie. The
flat round *Cap*, in it ſelfe conſidered as a Geome-
tricall figure, is far more worthy than the ſquare,
according to that ground in the *Mathematicks, fi-
gurarum ſpærica eſt optima,* and in *Hieroglyphickes,*
is a ſymbol of eternity, and perfection, & a reſem-
blance of the worlds rotunditie. But I will make
no encomium for caps. This I ſay, that as the
ſquare capp is retained not onely in the *Vniuerſi-
ties,* but alſo abroad among vs, as well by Eccle-
ſiaſticall perſons in high places, as by Iudges of the
Land, ſo the round capp being but a note in *London,* of Apprentiſes, and Citizens of *London,* as it is
of *Students, Barreſters, Benchers,* and *Readers,* in
the Innes of Court, ſo the wearing thereof by
Londoners cannot be a reproach, but an ornament.
But *communis error facit ius,* and how freely ſoeuer
theſe thoughts come from me out of abundant

loue

loue to the preferuation of vertue in that moft honorable City, which ciuill difcipline is ableft to
doe, yet as much pietie as it is to wifh the beft, fo
great is the vanity to thinke to ftoppe the generall
ftreame of predominant cuftome by priuate wi-
fhes. *Apprentifes* moreouer, and Citizens, becaufe
they are alwaies conuerfant in the light of action,
and concourfe, and not fhut vp in Colledges for
ftudies fake, may thinke by this contrary way the
more to honor their Citie, and to enioy thefelues.

12 Well may they in the meane time blufh at
their temeritie, who by teaching that *Apprentifes* are called Apprentifes, as if they were *pares
emptitijs,* doe difhonour and highly wrong the
excellent old policie of this land. For they (as much
as lyeth in the credit of their words) moft dange-
roufly difcourage flourifhing *Induftrie,* who caft
fuch an afperfion vpon any ciuill profeffion, and
order of men (affembled to vphold a kingdome
by comerce, according to Iuftice) as the leaft conceipt of fo hatefull a note as bondage. And if it
be temeritie to caft it vpon any renowned, or
other corporation vniuftly, it is fingular iniquitie
(let it not be called madneffe) to lay it vpon *London,* which fhines among all Cities within the
Empire of *Britain.* ———*velut inter ignes;*
                              Luna minores ———

The Contents of this fourth part.

1 *THe Author meanes not to erect a new* Babylon *by confounding degrees.* Horaces *monster. The common lawes distinction.*

2 *Citizens as Citizens not Gentlemen, but a particular species. The Gentleman the naturall subiect of all Nobilitie. The Authors meaning explained. Encouragement of honest* Industrie. Ius annulorum, *that among the* Romans, *which bearing of Armes among vs. The causes compared. The distinction of a meere Citizen. Disparagement of* Wards *how to bee vnderstood in this case. King* Edward *the first his displeasure an efficient of what effects. Armories to symbolise with the first bearers quality. Antiquities sacred care in point of ennoblements.*

3 *The Authors Apostrophe to Fathers, whether they be Gentlemen borne, or not. No cause why the Great should be ashamed of City-beginnings. Martiall vertue principal owner of Armories. The Chamber of the King.*

4 *Kings of* England *ennoble the Companies of* London *with their persons, by a singular fauour.* Henrie *the seuenth his admirable sociabilitie, or configuration of himselfe to popular formes.* Clothworkers *his late Maiesties brotherhood.*

5 London

5 London-Companies *denominated of their* Monopolies, *but not embased thereby. Of* Circensian-*games and colors.* Plinius *his complaint. Gentlemens meanes if properly entituled are as meane as* London-Mysteries. *Nor, in that respect, any great disparilitie betweene Countrey, and Citie-Gentlemen.*

6 *The Eccllipticke line of* Londons *Zodiacke. The minde, and not names is essentiall to qualifications.*

7 *The Authors second Apologie for his meaning in this case. His scope to beate downe iniurious vanity, not to wrong vocations.* London Companies *best so called as they are. The first* Roman *Consul, not being a* Patrician, *free of* Butchers. *Where Maiestie is, there can be no basenesse. The glorie of wit, and armes due to* London.

8 *All honest natures loue glorie, and no glorie good but as subordained to God.*

The

The fourth Part.

Hough thus I haue been the Aduocate, and Defender of the credit of the City, yet defire I not to be miftaken. For it is very far from my thoughts, by this Apologie, or patronifation, to confound degrees in commonweale, fo to fet vp as it were a new *Babylon* of mine owne. I am not ignorant therefore, that Citizens, as Citizens, are not Gentlemen, but Cizens; To hold otherwife were to take one order, or degree of men out of the Realme, or like *Horaces* monfter (a mans head, and a birds bodie) to create a thing which had halfe one, and halfe another, and our lawes giue a proper name both to the tenure, and perfon, calling the tenure of Citizens in Cities, *Burgage,* and their perfons, Burgenfes, among whom the more eminent of them in *London* had of old not onely the honour of the title of Citizens, or Burgeffes, but of *Barons* alfo.

2 The ordinarie Citizen therefore, is of a degree beneath the nieere Gentlemen, as the Gentleman is among vs in the loweft degree, or claffe of Nobilitie in *England.* And all
Citizens

Citizens as Citizens,yea,the Lord Maior himſelfe, ſimply as a Citizen, is not a Gentleman , but Burgenſis. As the greateſt Princes, and Deſpots that euer were,or euer ſhall be in the world,con-ſidered in their firſt naturall condition,are at moſt but *Ingenui*,or free-borne, in which reſpect all are equall,for *omnes natura æquales,* and their firſt ciuill degree,or generall ſtate, which either compre-hends all the orders of Nobilitie, or is capable of them,is among vs the Gentleman. In which re-ſpect he who ſhall ſay, That this or that King,or Emperour is a Gentleman, ſpeakes rightly,and as the thing is. For Gentleman is the title, about which all other titles,as they concerne honor,and conueigh no iuriſdiction,are put as robes and or-naments. This therefore is my meaning ; That ſome Citizens may be a Citizen, and yet truely a Gentleman, as one, and the ſame man may in ſe-ueral reſpects be both a Lord and Tenant.Citizen in regard of his encorporation in *London*, Gentle-man in regard of birth, or of Armories aſſigned for encouragement of *Induſtrie,*to ennoble his ho-neſt riches and titles of honor, or worſhip,in that City,whereof he is a qualified member. Neither is the communication of rewards, which conſiſt of painted diſtinctiós, compoſed according to the
receiued

receiued rules of *Heraldrie*, iniurious to ancient
Gentrie any more then the promiscuous permission of wearing gold-rings on their fingers alike
tofreed-men, as to freemen, granted by the Emperour in the authentickes: the reason of gold-rings
among *Romanes*, and of Armories among vs being the same. Nor is it a new thing in our Commonweale, that speciall Citizens, not borne to
armories, but the sonnes of yeomen, or not of
Gentlemen, should haue armes assigned them.
For there is perhaps scarce any record of Armes
granted in *England* more ancient then testimonies
in the Halles of *London*, that speciall Citizens haue
bin honourd with particular bearings. And these
are aduanced vpon the Lord Maiors day by the
speare-men of that companie of which his Lord-
ship is a member, not all of them specially giuen
of old, but some vndoubtedly borne by right of
blood, as descendents of Gentlemen, but other
againe as vndoubtedly assigned for excellency in City-Arts. Of which number there are
at this day not a few, whose *seri nepotes* whose
great-grand-childrens children are reputed amóg
the oldest and best families of their Shires, without any relation to *London*, which notwithstanding raised them. Hence it followes, that as an
Apprentise being a Gentleman-borne remaineth

a Gentleman, which addition of splendor, and title, as God blesseth his labours, so a worthy Citizen is capable of honor and Armes, notwithstanding his Apprentiship. And by this distinction made betweene a Citizen meerely as a Citizen, and of a Citizen, as hee may also be a Gentleman, that obiection which some bring out of a Statute enacted vnder one of our Kings, which forbidding the disparagement offered by the *Guardian* to marie the *Ward* borne gentle, to a *Burgensis,* may easily bee salued and answered. For in that Statute the word *Burgensis* is spoken in the natiue, and more narrow sense thereof, that is of one who is simply *Burgensis,* without any consideration of him as hee may otherwise bee a Gentleman, Esquire, or Knight, which in some places happens, as in the famous corporation of *Droit Wiche* in *Worcestershire.* But howsoeuer, certainely *Burgensis* here nothing concernes Citizens of *London,* who by an excellency of their calling had the honor in antiquity to beare the name of Barons, and were styled so; and weighing that, the Citizen is a distinct degree from *Burgensis,* and aboue it; and therfore that law concernes them not. For the proofe of their title to the appellation of Barons, by way of Hexoche (as artists in eloquence call

it)

it) moſt famous is that place in the Hiſtories of *Mathew Paris*, where ſpeaking of the Londoners of his time, vnder King *Henry* the third, theſe words are eminent in him : *Londonienſes quos propter ciuitatis dignitatem, & ciuium antiquitatem, Barones conſueuimus appellare.* As for the diſtinct degree of a Citizen from a *Burgenſis* , that appeares in this, that the City of *London* doth not ſend Burgeſſes to the Parliament, but Knights, or Citizens; and the enumeration of the rankes is cleare in a Statute of King *Richard* the ſecond, enacted the fift yeare of his raigne, and the fourth Chapter of the ſame, where they are, *(ount, Baron, Banneret, Cheualier de Counte, Citizen de Citie, Burgeis de Burgh.* The Princes before that time, but ſpecially the Princes following (as the worthineſſe of Citizens inuited) did ennoble them exceedingly, and continue more and more ſo to doe. Yet, in conferring Armes, and arguments of honor vpon Cizens, not borne Genlemen, reaſon requireth that they ſhould not haue coats of the faireſt bearing aſſigned to them, but ſuch as either in Canton, Chiefe, Border, or otherwiſe might carie ſome teſtimonie, marke, or ſigne to ſhew the Art by which they were aduanced, as Merchant-Aduenturers to beare Anchors, Grocers Cloues,

H 2

Cloth-

Clothworkers a Tezel, Merchantaylors a robe,
and fo forth ; which thofe Gentlemen ought in
honeftie,and thankfulneffe to choofe,and not only to accept ; and rather ftriue to match the beft in
goodneffe, and worth of fpirit then in the filent
tokens of it. Pofteritie thriuing, there may then
fome change be alfo made in the coat for the better. Specially confidering what pretty riddance
hath beene in our times made of furcharges in armories granted about the end of King *Henry* the
eight; what encroachments vpon old Gentlemens rights, by new ones, becaufe their names
onely haue beene the fame;and many other inuentions to blanch or beautifie newneffe. According
to which notion and dictamen, coats of Armes
haue beene deliuered from their originall defor-
mities, furfets, and furcharges, by their proper
Phyfitian,the prouinciall King of Armes; So Sir
Thomas Kitfons of *Suffolk*, whofe Chief,now fimply gold,was heretofore ouerladen with three o-
greffes, and they with an Anchor (the badge or
argument of the originall) and two Lyons ram-
pant argent; as at this houre is publikely extant to
be feene in *Trinitie* Hall at *Cambridge*, whereunto
he was a benefactor : and befides that Gentle-
mans, the coat armours of fome of the Peeres of
this

this land,and of others alſo,not a few: very many
more needing the like reliefe, or remedie.   The
rule of proportion ſeemes diligently obſerued in
antiquitie among vs, where the principall, and
moſt noble charges, and formes of Armories
were not appropriated but to analogicall compe-
tencies of honourable qualitie.

3 Such therefore being the nature of *Apprentiſhip,*and ſuch the condition of *Citizens* eſtate,as to
the purpoſes of honor,and armes,let *Fathers* who
are Gentleman put their children , who are not
rather inclining to Armes, or letters, to *Apprentiſhip,*that is to ſay, to the diſcipline, and Art of honeſt gaine,giuing them a title of being ſomewhat
in our Countrey. For it is a vocation ſimply honeſt, and may proue a ſtay to poſteritie, and giue
credit to their names, when licentious and cor-
rupted eldeſt ſonnes haue ſold their birth-rights
away. For albeit many Citizens thriue not, but
breake,yet thoſe fathers, or ſuch who are in place
of Fathers, worke more probably,who put their
children, or Orphans into a certaine method of
life,then others who leaue them at large. And as
ſome riotous, fooliſh, or vnfortunate Citizens
miſcarrie, ſo ten to one more yonger brethren in
the Country.And fathers,ſuch of you are not gen-

tlemen,put your children to be *Apprentifes*, that fo
as God may bleffe their iuft, true, and vertuous
induftrie,they may found a new family,and both
raife themfelues and theirs to the precious and
glittering title of Gentlemen bearing Armes law-
fully. For which caufe no Lord, nor Peere of
this Land, who may perchance owe his worldly eftate, and as well the completiue, as the fun-
damentall greatneffe, or amplitude of meanes, to
fuch as haue beene Citizens of *London*; nor thofe
other,whofe originalls were from cheualrie,and
martiall feruice(the moft pure, and proper Nobleffe of all, as to the purpofe of bearing Armes)
and yet fince haue beene mixt with Citie-races,
ought to thinke it the leaft difparagement to
owne their benefactors and anceftors , Citizens
of *London*. On the other part it will worthily
well become them , freely and thankfully to acknowledge fo honeft originalls, and accefsion
to originalls, as all this Realme from thence is
filled with. Becaufe among them the vertues of
commutatiue iuftice, and of commendable induftrie flourifh, and, the finewes of warre, and
peace, abundance of treafure, are ftored vp, as
in the Chamber of the King.

4 Which acknowledgment, befides that it is in
the

the lawes of honor, an act of bounden duty, they
may the rather take it for a glorie, becaufe our
Princes haue vouchfafed to be incorporated; as
members of feuerall Companies in the Citie,
comming thereby as it were vnder that banner.
Nor onely fo, but *Henrie* the feuenth (whom all
of vs will eafily confeffe to haue well enough vn-
derftood what he did) is credibly faid to haue
beene in perfon, at the election of *Mafter* & *Wardens,* and himfelfe to haue fitten openly among
them in a gowne of crimfon veluet, Citie-fafhi-
on, with a Citizens hood of veluet on his fhoul-
ders *a la mode de Londres,* vpon their folemne feaft-
day, in the common hall of his Company, *Mer-
chantailers.* Moreouer, his grand-childe, Queene
Elizabeth (no way inferior to her anceftor in high
pollicie) was free of *Mercers.* Laftlie (which is
more to our prefent purpofe) our late dread Soueraigne himfelfe King *Iames* more learned then
they both (though learning hath beene a Royall
abilitie in our ancient Princes, & fo flourifhing in
Sebert, King of *Eaft-England,* that our venerable
countreyman BEDE, affirmes him to haue been,
per omnia doctifsimus) encorporated himfelfe into
one the moft important fociety of this kingdome
Clothworkers, as men dealing in the principall and
noblest

nobleſt *Staplewares* of all theſe Ilands; wooll, and cloath.

5 Nor let the names of Companies, becauſe they ſeeme not to ſound honorably enough as appellations of degrees in Gentry, and Nobility, auert the mind from them as things ignoble and vnworthy the dignity of generous diſpoſitions, a thing erronicuſly holden in *Fernes Blazon* of *Gentry.* For all renowned Cities euer had in them *ᴠrbana nobilitas,* and yet their citizens could not but bee diſtributed into orders, tribes, or titles of profeſsions, yea ſometimes alſo in their games. For the *Circenſian* companies in *Rome,* called *factiones,* that is to ſay, companies, and denominated from the ſeuerall colors of their ſeueral clothings, *White, ſlew, greene,* and *red,* to which *Domitian* added two other *purple,* and *gold,* were the ſpeciall delights and exerciſes of Prince & people; which grew to ſuch exceſſe, no longer after then in *Traians* time, that *Plinius ſecundus* held it a matter worthy of his complaint, and cenſure, as in one of his Epiſtles is extant, where he ſaith *nunc panno fauent, nunc pannum amant.* Againe, ſuch of the *Gentry,* who liue not in the citie, and doe moſt of all eleuate themſelues with contempt of others in reſpect of the Arts, and wayes of maintenance, were they but

but incorporated vnder the true titles of their meanes, in which we will not fpeake of the prodigious eating vp of whole houfes, townes, and people, by a thoufand wicked deuifes proper to the myfterie of depopulation (againft whole confuming works fo many ftatutes of this land haue long time warred in vaine) the names of thofe citie-brotherhoods, or Companies would eafilie found, in a moft curious eare, full out as faire, and well. *Corne, Cattle, Butter, Cheefe, Hay, Wood, Wooll, Coles,* and the like, the materialls of their maintenance, all of them infeparable to Countrey-Commonweales, and without which they can no more fubfift then *Drapers,* as *Drapers* without cloath, *Glodfmiths,* as *Goldfmiths* without Iewc:s, or plate, and fo forth. Neither doth it create any great odds in this point touching honour betweene parties in this difpute, that Gentlemen, by their officers, as Bailiffes, Reeues, or the like, doe order their affaires for their more eafe, & dignities. For befides, that the wifeft among them exercife that fuperintendency in their owne perfons, fo herein the worthy Citizen is no way behind, difpatching his bufineffes by Factors, Iourneymen, or expert *Apprentifes,* referuing onely to himfelfe the oueruiew, and controll all their doings. Citie-no-

I blefle

bleſſe ſo apparent,that the Knights or Gentlemen of *Rome*, profeſſing Merchandiſe, and others among them that way bent, had their Hall, or ſeat of their Colledge, or companie vpon Mount *Capitoline* it ſelfe, dedicated to their patron Deity , or tutelarie God-head,*Mercurie.* Other encorporated ſocieties there alſo were,as Goldſmiths, and the reſt,who liued ſo far from being excluded out of the power of common-weale, or from honors, and ſignes of nobleneſſe, that they had right in ſome caſes euen to ouertop the Lords, and out of their owne body to chooſe not only Conſuls,but euen Dictators alſo,their ſuper-ſoueraigne & moſt abſolute Magiſtrate before their Emperors times. Yea ſo mighty were they growne in reſpect of elections and negatiue authoritie, that *Clodius* to be reuenged vpon *Cicero*,left his owne rancke of Patritians,and Lords,and turned Commoner.

6 To conclude, ſuch Gentlemen are much deceiued, which no ſooner heare one named to be of this, or that Societie, or Colledge of trade in *London*, as of *Grocers*,*Haberdaſhers*,*Fiſhmongers*,or of any other of the twelue principall *Monopolies* (the Zodiacke of the citie, in whoſe Eclipticke line their Lord Maior muſt euer runne his yeares courſe) but they forthwith entertaine a low conceit

ceit of the parties quality, as too too much beneath
their owne ranck, and order, without further ex-
aminatiõ; *when it often happens, that he who is titular-*
lie of this, or that Fraternity, neuer was bred vp in it,
nor vnderstands any more what it meanes then the re-
motest Gentleman, their Masters themselues hauing been
Merchants, or of other profession of life diuerse from their
title, vnder which they are marshall'd, the law of the
citie imposing an absolute necessity that all who
are free of the city should cary the name of some
one, or other of their brotherhoods. Againe, what
doe the constellations of heauen shine the worse,
or the lesse, because they carrie the names of
Ramm, of a *Water-bearer,* of *Fishes,* and so forth?
Or how many the fewer are their seuerall lights
for that? Answerably to which I say, that if the
parties mind be adorn'd with the starre-lights of
vertue and honor, what basenesse is it for him to
bee marshall'd vnder any of the names compre-
hending one, or other of the honest Arts of
worldly life?

    7 In disputing thus, let me not be thought
to set vp an enuious comparison betweene these
two worshipfull degrees, or qualificatiõs of men.
That is very farre from me. For it must euer bee
granted, to the authority of general opinion foun-

ded vpon cuſtome among vs, that the true Coun-
trey-Eſquire *cæteris paribus*, is in his proper place
before the Citie-Eſquire, which with the perpe-
tuall clauſe beforeſaid of *cæteris paribus* holds alſo,
throughout the other degrees of the inferior Nobleſſe in *England*. I reaſon here, as reaſon bids, not
againſt the right, or dignities of perſons either as
in parallell, or as in diſparagement, but againſt the
vanity, and offences riſing out of cauſeleſſe elatiō,
and arrogance, and againſt their errours, who
not vnderſtanding the things of their owne countrey, are indeed meere *Meteoroſcopers*, and houer in
the clowdy region of admiration vpon rude, and
vnlearned fanſies, for which cauſe as minds needing to be healed, ſo would I ſincerely that they
were healed. Such are theirs, who would perhaps think the Companies, or Monopolies of the
citie more worthy of their acknowledgement, if
where now they are denominated of ſome particular ware, or craft, they were named of *Eagles,*
Vultures, Lions, Beares, Panthers, Tygers, or ſo forth,
as the ſeuerall orders of the Noble in *Mexico* (wᶜʰ
Ioſephus Acoſta writes) vnder their Emperor : yet
much better, becauſe more truly, theſe fellowſhips
of *London* cary the names of men as they haue vocations in profeſſions, which onely men can exe-
cute.

cute. Or they would peraduenture thinke more
noblie of them, if thofe focieties were denominated of *Eyes*, *eares*, *hands*, *feet*, or of other
members, as *Philoſtratus*, in the life of that impo-
ſtor *Apollonius Tianæus*, ſaith, the officers, and in-
ſtruments of a Philoſophical King in *India* were-
But as thoſe were called of their King his *eyes*,
eares, and ſo forth, ſo haue theſe myſteries ſome
one, or other profeſſor in each among them, from
the higher trade to the loweſt eminently deſigned
out with the addition of King, as the Kings Mer-
cer, the Kings Draper, and ſo forth. Againe, how
much more worthy the whole is then the parts,
becauſe the parts are in the whole, ſo by that argument it is more honourable to be marſhall'd as a
man among focieties of ciuill men, then to be di-
ſtinguiſht by alluſions to particular members. At
leaſtwiſe, thoſe ſingular Gentlemen might certain-
in their moſt contempt of the City reméber that
of *Plato, Nemo Rex non ex ſeruis, nemo non ſeruus ex
Regibus;* and that alſo rare and reall worth may
bee in the perſons of Citizens themſelues, ſee-
ing *Terentius* (Conſul of old *Rome*, with that noble *Paulus Æmilius*) was free of the Butchers company, and our *Walworth* Lord Maior of old *London* was free of the Fiſhmongers. And they were

not onely the Lords, Knights, and Gentlemen of
Rome, who had voice in election of their principall yearly Magiftrates, but euen handycrafts-men
and Artificers, as is moft manifeft by that place of
Saluft in his *Iugurthine* warre, where *Marius* was
chofen Conful, by the fpeciall affection of that fort
of *Roman* Citizens, who (faith he) *fua neceffaria
poft illius honorem ducebant,* preferred his election
by their voices, before the trades by which they
earnd their liuings. Finally, they may reméber, that
in the pofterity of Citizens many right noble, and
worthy Gentlemen are often found, and that, befides the vniuerfall mixture with Citie-races tho-
row the Kingdom, it may not be denyed that true
noblefs fhineth oftenvery bright among thé. For
they are Companies of free Citizens, in which, fo-
ueraigne Maiefty it felfe is incorporated, making
them at onceto be facred as it were, and certainly
magnificent. For euen as where the Sun is, there is
no darknes, fo where foueraign Princes are inter-
reffed parties, there is no bafenes. And as the Philo-
fophers Medicine purgeth vileft metals, turning
all to gold, fo the operation of Princes intention
to ennoble Societies with his perfonall prefence,
tranfmetalls the fubiect, and clearly takes away all
ignobilitie. Which things as they are moft true in
                                          London,

London,fo,for that,the Emperour *Conftantinus magnus* (if our ancient *Fitz Stephan* reports the right) *Henry* King of *England*, fonne of king *Henry* the fecond, and that braue great Prince *Edward* the firft,and whofoeuer elfe,were borne in the Citie, they giue to it the glory of Armes : and *Ieffrey Chaucer*, Sir *Thomas* Moore knight, with others borne in *London*, communicate thereunto the glorie of wits and letters. To nourifh vp both which moft excellent titles to reall nobilitie in the Citie, the Artillery-yard, and *Greffam* Colledge were inftituted.

8 Thus this queftion of Honor, and Armes, vndertaken at the inftance of intereffed parties, but more for loue to that great Citie,and her children,being by Gods affiftance, and,as we hope, fufficiently difcuffed, the end of all is this, that albeit the loue of humane praife, and of outward fplendor in the markes, and teftimonies of it, are very vehement fires in all worthieft natures, yet haue they no beatitude,nor(fo to fay) felicitation, but onely as with referment to this of the bleffed Apoftle,   *Soli Deo Honor, & Gloria.*
Amen.

I haue viewed this booke,and perufed the fame, and finde nothing therein diffonant to reafon, or contrary to the Law of Honor or Armes.

William Segar *Garter princip.*
King of Armes.

Errata.

In the Epiſtle to the Maſters.

For iuice of ingratitude, *read* vice of ingratitude.

In the Epiſtle to the Prenttſes.

For preying, *read* prying.

For honourable (all, *read* honorable ſtrangers (all.

Page 5. *For* larger volume, *read* leger volume.

17. *For* diſcouſer, *read* diſcourſer.

19. *For* ciuill Art gouernment, *read* ciuill Art of gouernment.

ead. *For* moſt an- Art of encreaſe, *read* moſt ancient Art of encreaſe.

20. *For* a would, *read* as would.

23. *For* ouer ſla ue, *read* ouer his ſlaue.

38. *For* faſteth, *read* faſteſt.

51. *For* you are, *read* you as are.

55. *For* controll all *read* controll of all.

57. *For* Ramme, *read* a Ramme.

58. *For* certaine, *read* certainly.